Bond

UP TO *SPEED*
Maths
Tests and Papers

9–10 years

Paul Broadbent

Nelson Thornes

Published in 2013 by:
Nelson Thornes Ltd
Delta Place
27 Bath Road
CHELTENHAM
GL53 7TH
United Kingdom

13 14 15 16 17 / 10 9 8 7 6 5 4 3 2 1

A catalogue record for this book is available from the British Library

ISBN 978 1 4085 1889 2

Page make-up and illustrations by GreenGate Publishing Services, Tonbridge, Kent

Printed in China by 1010 Printing International Ltd

Introduction

What is Bond?

The Bond *Up to Speed* series is a new addition to the Bond range of assessment papers, the number one series for the 11+, selective exams and general practice. Bond *Up to Speed* is carefully designed to support children who need less challenging activities than those in the regular age-appropriate Bond papers, in order to build up and improve their techniques and confidence.

How does this book work?

The book contains two distinct sets of papers, along with full answers and a Progress Chart:

- Focus tests, accompanied by advice and directions, are focused on particular (and age-appropriate) Maths question types encountered in the 11+ and other exams. The questions are deliberately set at a less challenging level than the standard *Assessment Papers*. Each Focus test is designed to help a child 'catch' their level in a particular question type, and then gently raise it through the course of the test and the subsequent Mixed papers.

- Mixed papers are longer tests containing a full range of Maths question types. These are designed to provide rigorous practice with less challenging questions, perhaps against the clock, in order to help children acquire and develop the necessary skills and techniques for 11+ success.

Full answers are provided for both types of test in the middle of the book.

Some questions may require a ruler or protractor. Calculators are not permitted.

How much time should the tests take?

The tests are for practice and to reinforce learning, and you may wish to test exam techniques and working to a set time limit. Using the Mixed papers, we would recommend that your child spends 60 minutes answering the 50 questions in each paper.

You can reduce the suggested time by 5 minutes to practise working at speed.

Using the Progress Chart

The Progress Chart can be used to track Focus test and Mixed paper results over time to monitor how well your child is doing and identify any repeated problems in tackling the different question types.

Look at the value of each digit in a number:

41 735

40 000 + 1000 + 700 + 30 + 5

forty-one thousand seven hundred and thirty-five

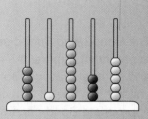

1 Write the number at each arrow on this number line.

4000   5000

2 Write these numbers in order of size, starting with the smallest.

6412	6900
4395	4953

_____   _____   _____   _____

Smallest →

3 Round 4755 m to the nearest 100 m. _____ m

Read these and write each as a number.

4 thirty-four thousand four hundred and twelve _____

5 sixteen thousand and eight _____

6 Write the number that is 100 more than 67 052. _____

Decimal numbers are any numbers made from the digits 0 to 9.
A decimal point is used to separate whole numbers from decimals.

This shows tenths.

0.3 is the same as $\frac{3}{10}$

This shows hundredths.

0.03 is the same as $\frac{3}{100}$

Circle the number that is the same value as each fraction.

7 $\frac{7}{10}$ 70   7   0.7   0.07

8 $\frac{9}{100}$ 900   90   0.9   0.09

9 Write < or > to make this number sentence true.

10.16 _____ 10.9

10 Write this set of decimals in order, starting with the smallest.

     9.36   39.6   9.63   6.39

    _____ < _____ < _____ < _____

11 Round 3.56 kg to the nearest tenth. _____ kg

12 Complete these calculations.

62 ÷ 10 = _____

0.07 × 10 = _____

Write the missing numbers to complete these additions.

1
```
    5 6 3 ☐
  +  2 ☐ 4 6
    8 2 ☐ 8
```

2
```
    4 ☐ 4 8
  + 3 9 0 ☐
    8 5 ☐ 2
```

> When you add decimals, remember to line up the decimal points. The method is the same as with whole numbers.
>
> *Example*
>
> What is the total of 12.6, 3.5 and 2.93?
>
> ```
>     1 2 . 6
>        3 . 5
>   +    2 . 9 3
>     1 9 . 0 3
> ```

Complete these additions.

3
```
       7.3
      1 3.9
   +   8.5
   _____
```

4
```
     5 7.2
       6.2
   + 4 3.8
   _____
```

5 Write the total weight for this group of parcels. _____ kg

25.9 kg   23.7 kg   9.65 kg

Complete these calculations.

6
```
     9 3 0 6
   - 6 0 2 8
   _____
```

7
```
     7 1 9 4
   - 3 8 7 7
   _____
```

6

8 Joel bought a tennis racket for £32.65 and a tube of tennis balls for £6.80.

How much did he spend in total? £_____

How much change did he get from £50? £_____

Try using a number line to count on to find the difference between numbers.

Example

What is the difference between 17.8 and 26?

Draw a blank number line from 17.8 to 26. Count on to 18, then on to 26 to find the difference:

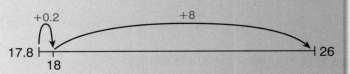

The difference is 8.2.

---

9 Find the difference between each pair of numbers.

26.7 ⊢————————⊣ 45   _____

19.6 ⊢————————⊣ 32   _____

10 Write the missing numbers on this difference grid.

−	2.5	3.1	6.7
1.4	1.1	_____	_____
5.6	_____	2.5	_____
7.3	_____	_____	_____

Look at these numbers.

13.7   21.8   19.6   27.3

11 What is the difference between the largest and smallest number? _____

12 Which two numbers have a difference of 2.2? _____ and _____

Now go to the Progress Chart to record your score!   Total   12

Try to learn all your tables facts. These are the facts that probably cause the most problems, so practise these until you know them:

9 × 6	4 × 7	6 × 7	3 × 8	4 × 8
6 × 8	7 × 8	4 × 9	7 × 9	8 × 9

1 This is a 'multiply by 4' machine.
Write the missing numbers in the chart.

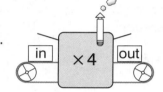

IN	3	8	___	10	___	4
OUT	12	___	28	___	24	___

2 There are six pencils in a box. How many pencils are there in eight boxes? _____

3 There are seven days in a week. How many days are there in nine weeks? _____

4 Write =, < or > to make each statement true.

18 ÷ 2 _____ 9   7 × 6 _____ 50   56 ÷ 7 _____ 6

With a grid method for multiplication, multiply each pair of numbers to complete the grid. Then add the numbers to find the total.

Example: What is 16 multiplied by 4?

×	10	6	
4	40	24	→ 64

5 Use this grid to multiply 18 by 7.

$$\begin{array}{c|c|c} \times & 10 & 8 \\ \hline 7 & & \end{array} \rightarrow \underline{\hspace{1cm}}$$

6 What is 48 multiplied by 3? _____

7 Here are some number cards.

Use two of these cards as digits to make a number that can be divided exactly by 9.

_____ _____

8 Tennis balls are sold in tubes of 4. How many balls will there be in 65 tubes? _____

9 A box holds 6 tins of dog food. How many boxes are needed for 48 tins? _____

If a number cannot be divided exactly it leaves a remainder.

What is 85 divided by 4 and what is the remainder?

$$\begin{array}{r} 2\ 1 \quad r\ 1 \\ 4\overline{)8\ 5} \\ -8\ 0 \\ \hline 5 \\ -4 \\ \hline 1 \end{array}$$ (4 × 20)
(4 × 1)

$85 \div 4 = 21$ remainder 1

Complete these calculations.

10 $5\overline{)6\ 7}$ **11** $3\overline{)5\ 8}$ **12** $4\overline{)9\ 5}$

Factors, multiples and prime numbers

Factors are those numbers that will divide exactly into other numbers. Factors of numbers can be put into pairs:

Factors of 15   →   (1, 15)   (3, 5)   15 has four factors.

Factors of 18   →   (1, 18)   (2, 9)   (3, 6)   18 has six factors.

1 Write the missing factors of 24.

24 → (1, 24)   (2, ____)   (3, ____)   (____, ____)

2 Circle the numbers that are factors of 12.

1   2   3   4   5   6   7   8   9   10   11   12

3 Write the factors of 49 in order, starting with the smallest.

____, ____, ____

A prime number only has two factors, 1 and itself. For example, 7 is a prime number as it can only be divided exactly by 1 and 7. The number 1 is not a prime number.

4 What are the first four prime numbers? ____   ____   ____   ____

5 After the number 2, every prime number is an odd number.

True or False? _____

A multiple is a number made by multiplying together two other numbers. For example, the multiples of 5 are 5, 10, 15, 20, and so on.

6 Circle the numbers that are multiples of both 2 and 3.

12   15   6   9   10   18   24

7 Write each of these numbers in the correct place on the Venn diagram.

30   **25**   **18**   **16**

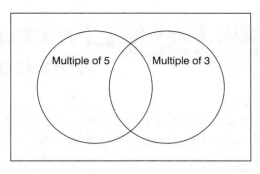

8 I am thinking of a number. It is a multiple of 4 and a multiple of 7. It is between 50 and 60. What is the number I am thinking of? _____

9 Circle all the multiples of 3 and underline all the factors of 15.

8   10   15   9   5   3   30

10 Write each number in the correct place on this Carroll diagram.

6   8   10   16

	Multiple of 4	Not a multiple of 4
Factor of 24	_____	_____
Not a factor of 24	_____	_____

11 Complete these multiplications.

$1 \times 1 =$ _____

$2 \times 2 =$ _____

$3 \times 3 =$ _____

A number multiplied by itself gives a square number.

$3 \times 3 = 9$

$3^2 = 9$

12 Complete these calculations.

$4^2 =$ _____

$5^2 =$ _____

$6^2 =$ _____

Equivalent fractions have the same value, even though they may look different.

$\frac{3}{12} = \frac{1}{4}$

$\frac{3}{12}$ is simplified to $\frac{1}{4}$

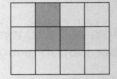

Write the fraction of each shape that is shaded. Simplify each fraction.

1

2

3

   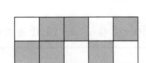

_____   _____   _____

Circle **two** fractions that have the same value as the first fraction.

4 $\frac{2}{3}$ $\frac{5}{9}$ $\frac{8}{12}$ $\frac{4}{8}$ $\frac{6}{9}$

5 $\frac{3}{10}$ $\frac{9}{20}$ $\frac{4}{15}$ $\frac{6}{20}$ $\frac{30}{100}$

6 Use ticks to complete this chart.

	Greater than $\frac{1}{2}$	Less than $\frac{1}{2}$
0.45		
0.54		

7 Draw lines to match each fraction to its equivalent decimal.

$\frac{1}{2}$ $\frac{3}{4}$ $\frac{2}{5}$ $\frac{3}{10}$ $\frac{1}{4}$ $\frac{9}{10}$

0.25   0.75   0.5   0.4   0.9   0.3

8 Circle the smallest decimal and underline the largest decimal.

0.4   0.25   0.6   0.01   0.1   0.7

To change fractions to percentages, make them out of 100. This means you need to find the equivalent fraction with the denominator 100.

Example

$\frac{3}{10}$ is equivalent to $\frac{30}{100}$ so $\frac{3}{10}$ = 30%

To change a percentage to a fraction, make it a fraction out of 100 and then simplify it.

Example

5% is $\frac{5}{100}$, which is the same as $\frac{1}{20}$

> % is the percentage sign: per cent means 'out of 100'.

---

9 What fraction of this rectangle is shaded? Simplify the fraction. _____

10 Circle the percentage of this rectangle that is shaded.

20%   80%   40%   75%   60%

11 Shade more of the squares so that 80% of the rectangle is shaded in total.

12 Look at these fractions.

$\frac{1}{5}$ $\frac{7}{10}$ $\frac{1}{3}$ $\frac{3}{4}$ $\frac{2}{5}$

Which fraction is equivalent to $\frac{3}{9}$? _____

Which fraction has the same value as 20%? _____

Which fraction has the same value as 0.75? _____

Now go to the Progress Chart to record your score!   Total ◯ 12

Focus test 6   Sequences

A sequence is a list of numbers in a pattern.

You can often find the rule for a sequence by looking at the difference between the numbers.

What is the next number in this sequence?

   35   39   43   47   _____

Each number is 4 more than the previous number, so the next number is 51.

The rule is 'add 4'.

What is the next number in each sequence?

1 54   45   36   27   _____

2 145   195   245   295   _____

3 Write the missing numbers on this grid.

1	2	3	4	5			8	9	10
20	19				15	14	13		11
21	22	23			26	27		29	
40		38		36			33		31
	42				46		48		50

Write the missing number in each sequence.

4 2.5   3.1   _____   4.3   4.9

5 3   0   _____   −6   −9

6 What are the next two numbers in this sequence?

16   31   46   61   _____   _____

7 What is the rule for this sequence?

8   5   2   −1   −4   −7

The rule is _____

8 Will −15 be in the sequence above? Yes or No? _____

Write the missing numbers in each sequence.

9 0.7   1.2   _____   2.2   2.7   _____

10 $\frac{1}{4}$ $\frac{1}{2}$ _____   1 $1\frac{1}{4}$ _____

11 What is the rule for this sequence?

1   2   4   8   16   32

The rule is _____

12 What are the next three numbers in this sequence?

150   300   450   600   _____   _____   _____

Focus test 7   Shapes and angles

> Here are the properties of different triangles:
>
> | **Equilateral** | **Isosceles** | **Right-angled** | **Scalene** |
> |---|---|---|---|
> | • 3 equal sides
• 3 equal angles | • 2 equal sides
• 2 equal angles | • one angle is a right-angle | • no equal sides
• no equal angles |

Name these triangles.

1

2

3

_____   _____   _____

4 An isosceles triangle can also be a right-angled triangle.

   True or False? _____

5 Cross out the shape that is **not** a quadrilateral.

6 How many lines of symmetry are there on a regular hexagon? _____

7 Draw a symmetrical quadrilateral on this grid.
   Show the lines of symmetry with a dotted line.

3-D shapes are made up of faces, edges and vertices (corners).

This square-based pyramid has 5 faces, 8 edges, 5 vertices.

8 Complete this chart.

Name of shape	Number of faces	Number of vertices	Number of edges
Cube	_____	_____	_____
Tetrahedron	_____	_____	_____

9 Write the name of each shape.

  _____

  _____

10 How many faces does a cuboid have? _____

11 Look at this trapezium and complete the chart.

Type of angle	Acute	Obtuse	Right
Number of angles	_____	_____	_____

A protractor is used to measure the size of an angle. It is a good idea to estimate the angle first and then measure it.

12 Measure these angles accurately with a protractor.

Angle *a* = _____ °

Angle *b* = _____ °

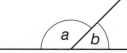

These are special types of angles to remember:

straight line	180°		acute angle	less than 90°	
right angle	90°		obtuse angle	between 90° and 180°	

Now go to the Progress Chart to record your score!   Total   12

17

Focus test 8 — Area and perimeter

The area of a shape is the amount of surface that it covers. You can find the area of shapes by counting squares. Area is usually measured in square centimetres or square metres, written as cm^2 and m^2. Always remember to write this at the end of the measurement.

The area of a rectangle is length x width.

Example

Area = 3 cm x 4 cm

= 12 square centimetres (12 cm^2)

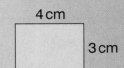

4 cm

3 cm

1 Draw a shape on this grid with an area of 15 squares.

2 What is the area of this shape?
_____ squares

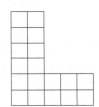

3 A rectangle has an area of 48 square centimetres. One side is 6 cm long.

What is the length of the other side?

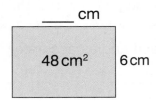

_____ cm

48 cm^2 6 cm

4 Calculate the area of this rectangle.

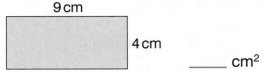

9 cm

4 cm

_____ cm^2

5 Draw a square on this grid with an area of 25 cm^2. Use a ruler.

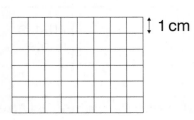

↕ 1 cm

The perimeter of a shape is the distance all the way around the edge. If the shape has straight sides, add up the lengths of all the sides. You can work out the perimeter of a rectangle by totalling the length and width and then doubling the total.

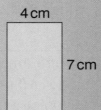

4cm

7cm

- Add together the length and width:
  7cm + 4cm = 11cm

- Double 11cm is 22cm.

- So the perimeter of rectangle is 22cm.

Calculate the perimeter of each rectangle.

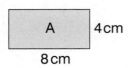

A   4cm

8cm

B   7cm

5cm

6 Perimeter of A = _____ cm

7 Perimeter of B = _____ cm

8 Which shape has the larger area, A or B? _____

What is the area and perimeter of the room shown in this diagram?

9 Area = _____ m²

10 Perimeter = _____ m

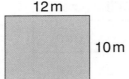

12m

10m

11 A square has an area of 9cm² and a perimeter of 12cm.

What is the length of one side of this square? _____ cm

12

A 6m

4m

B 5m

5m

C 3m

8m

Draw a line to join the two shapes with the same size area.

Tick the two shapes with the same length perimeter.

Length, weight (or mass) and capacity are all measured using different units.

Length	1 metre (m) = 100 centimetres (cm) 1 cm = 10 millimetres (mm) 1 kilometre (km) = 1000 m
Weight	1 kilogram (kg) = 1000 grams (g)
Capacity	1 litre (l) = 1000 millilitres (ml)

Once you know these then you can convert from one unit to another by multiplying or dividing by 10, 100 or 1000.

Examples

35 mm = 3.5 cm   2.3 kg = 2300 g   1500 ml = 1.5 litres

1   Convert each of these lengths to complete the table.

Metres	Centimetres	Millimetres
6.5 m	_____ cm	_____ mm
_____ m	720 cm	_____ mm
_____ m	_____ cm	3000 mm

2   How many millilitres are there in 4.8 litres? _____ ml

3   How many grams are there in 0.6 kilograms? _____ g

4   Which is heavier, $3\frac{1}{4}$ kg or 3400 g? _____

5   Write these lengths in order, starting with the shortest.

85 mm   **0.8 m**   **85 cm**   **8.5 m**

_____   _____   _____   _____

Shortest →

A scale is a row of marks to help us measure on a jug or ruler, for example. You need to read them accurately.

Look at the unit. Is it ml, cm, g...?

- If the level is in line with a mark, read off that number.
- If it is between numbers, work out what each mark means and count on or back.

Read the scales and write how much water is in each jug.

6
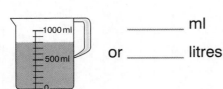
_____ ml

or _____ litres

7
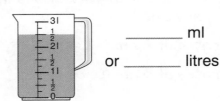
_____ ml

or _____ litres

8 Measure the sides of this triangle with a ruler. Measure two sides in millimetres and the other side to the nearest half centimetre.

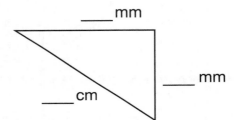
_____ mm

_____ mm

_____ cm

9 Draw an arrow on the scale to show 6.4 kg.

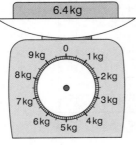

10 What is the most likely amount of water needed to fill a mug?

Circle the answer.

30 litres   3 litres

30 ml   300 ml

11 A train should arrive at 4:35pm but it is 20 minutes late. What time will the train actually arrive?

Write the time on the digital clock and draw the time on the clock face.

12 A film starts at 7:10pm and lasts for an hour and a half.

What time will the film finish? _____

Transformations and coordinates

Coordinates are used to show positions on a grid.

Coordinates are always pairs of numbers written in brackets and separated by a comma.

The number on the horizontal x-axis is written first, then the number on the vertical y-axis.

The coordinates of A are (−2, 4).

The coordinates of B are (5, 3).

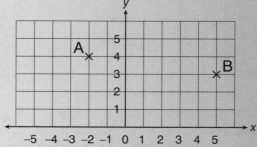

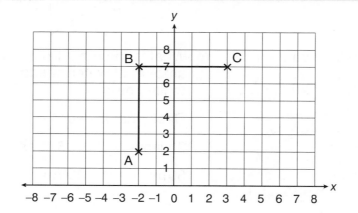

1 What are the coordinates of point A?   (_____ , _____)

2 What are the coordinates of point B?   (_____ , _____)

3 What are the coordinates of point C?   (_____ , _____)

4 A, B and C are three vertices of a square. Mark the missing fourth vertex with a cross and label it D. Join the vertices to make a square.

5 What are the coordinates of point D?   (_____ , _____)

6 Plot an isosceles triangle on this grid. Label the vertices A, B and C.

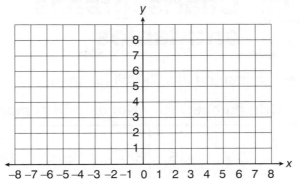

7 What are the coordinates of your triangle?

A → (_____, _____)   B → (_____, _____)   C → (_____, _____)

A shape can be moved in three ways.

- Rotation: the shape is rotated about a point, clockwise or anticlockwise.

- Reflection: this is sometimes called 'flipping over'.

- Translation: this is sliding the shape across, up, down or diagonally, without rotating or flipping over.

Write whether these shapes have been **translated**, **rotated** or **reflected**.

8   **9**   **10**

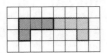   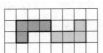   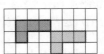

_____   _____   _____

This tile is used to make a pattern.

11 Has the tile been rotated, translated or reflected to make this pattern?

_____

12 Use the tile to make a different pattern. Have you used a translation, rotation or reflection?

_____

The numbers 1–20 have been written on this Carroll diagram.

	Odd number			Not an odd number		
Multiple of 3	3	9	15	6	12	18
Not a multiple of 3	1 11 19	5 13	7 17	2 10 20	4 14	8 16

1 Write these numbers in the correct place on the diagram.

21   **22**   **23**   **24**   **25**

Now look at the Carroll diagram with your numbers added and answer these questions.

2 How many numbers are both odd and multiples of 3? _____

3 How many numbers are not odd and not a multiple of 3? _____

4 How many numbers in total are not a multiple of 3? _____

To understand bar charts and other types of graphs, look carefully at the different parts of the graph before you look at the bars.

- Read the title. What is it about?
- Look at the axis labels. These explain the lines that go across and up.
- Work out the scale. Does it go up in 1s, 2s, 5s, 10s...?

The information from the Carroll diagram has been drawn on a block graph.

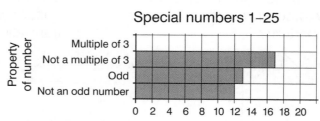

Special numbers 1–25

5 Count how many numbers are multiples of 3 and draw the missing block on this graph.

Use the information on the block graph to answer these questions.

6 How many numbers are even? _____

7 How many more odd numbers are there than even numbers? _____

8 How many odd and even numbers are there in total? _____

This is a conversion chart for changing litres into pints and pints into litres.

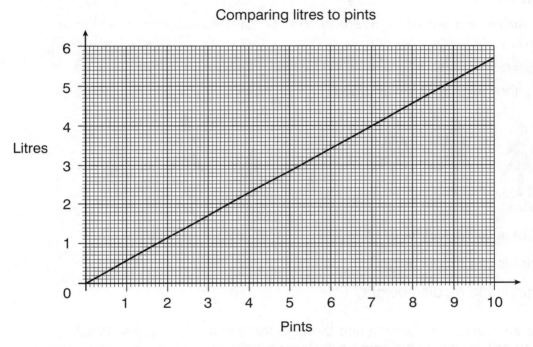

Comparing litres to pints

9 Approximately how many pints are the same as 4 litres? _____ pints

10 How many litres are about the same as $3\frac{1}{2}$ pints? _____ litres

11 How much is 1 pint to the nearest 100 ml? _____ ml

12 Which is greater, 5 pints or 5 litres? _____

Now go to the Progress Chart to record your score! Total ◯ 12

Mean, median, mode and probability

- The mode of a set of data is the item that occurs the most often.
- The median is the middle number in a set of numbers when arranged in order.
- The mean of a set of numbers is their total divided by the number of items.

These are the heights of seven trees.

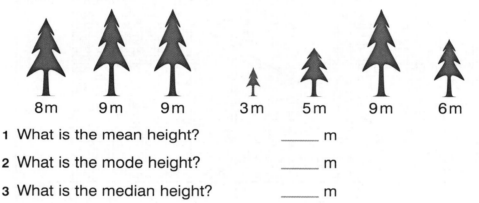

8m   9m   9m   3m   5m   9m   6m

1 What is the mean height? _____ m

2 What is the mode height? _____ m

3 What is the median height? _____ m

Two trees are cut down. Draw a line through the 3m and 6m trees. What is the median and mean of the remaining five trees?

4 What is the new median? _____ m

5 What is the new mean? _____ m

6 What is the chance of seeing a bird today? Underline the answer.

impossible   poor chance   even chance   good chance   certain

A probability scale can be used to show how likely an event is to happen.

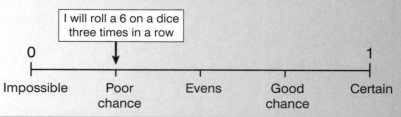

Focus test 1

1. 4200, 4830
2. 4395, 4953, 6412, 6900
3. 4800 m
4. 34 412
5. 16 008
6. 67 152
7. 0.7
8. 0.09
9. <
10. 6.39 < 9.36 < 9.63 < 39.6
11. 3.6 kg
12. 6.2, 0.7

Focus test 2

1.
$$\begin{array}{r} 563\mathbf{2} \\ +2646 \\ \hline 8278 \end{array}$$
2.
$$\begin{array}{r} 46\mathbf{4}8 \\ +3904 \\ \hline 8552 \end{array}$$
3. 29.7
4. 107.2
5. 59.25 kg
6. 3278
7. 3317
8. £39.45, £10.55
9. 18.3, 12.4
10.

−	2.5	3.1	6.7
1.4	1.1	**1.7**	**5.3**
5.6	**3.1**	2.5	**1.1**
7.3	**4.8**	**4.2**	**0.6**

11. 13.6
12. 21.8 and 19.6

Focus test 3

1.

IN	3	8	**7**	10	**6**	4
OUT	12	**32**	28	**40**	24	**16**

2. 48
3. 63
4. =, <, >
5. 126
6. 144
7. 27 or 72
8. 260
9. 8
10. 13 r 2
11. 19 r 1
12. 23 r 3

Focus test 4

1. (2, 12) (3, 8) (4, 6)

2. 1, 2, 3, 4, 6, 12
3. 1, 7, 49
4. 2, 3, 5, 7
5. True
6. 12, 6, 18, 24
7.

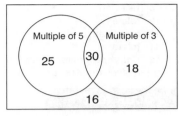

8. 56
9. 8 10 (15) (9) 5 (3) (30)
10.

	Multiple of 4	Not a multiple of 4
Factor of 24	8	6
Not a factor of 24	16	10

11. 1, 4, 9
12. 16, 25, 36

Focus test 5

1. $\frac{1}{3}$
2. $\frac{3}{5}$
3. $\frac{3}{4}$
4. $\frac{8}{12}, \frac{6}{9}$
5. $\frac{6}{20}, \frac{30}{100}$
6.

	Greater than $\frac{1}{2}$	Less than $\frac{1}{2}$
0.45		✓
0.54	✓	

7. $\frac{1}{2}$ and 0.5, $\frac{3}{4}$ and 0.75, $\frac{2}{5}$ and 0.4, $\frac{3}{10}$ and 0.3, $\frac{1}{4}$ and 0.25, $\frac{9}{10}$ and 0.9
8. (0.01), 0.7
9. $\frac{2}{5}$
10. 40%
11. *Check four more squares are shaded.*
12. $\frac{1}{3}, \frac{1}{5}, \frac{3}{4}$

Focus test 6

1. 18
2. 345

3.

1	2	3	4	5	**6**	**7**	8	9	10
20	19	**18**	**17**	**16**	15	14	13	**12**	11
21	22	23	**24**	**25**	26	27	**28**	29	**30**
40	**39**	38	**37**	36	**35**	**34**	33	**32**	31
41	42	**43**	**44**	**45**	46	**47**	48	**49**	50

4. 3.7
5. −3
6. 76, 91
7. subtract 3
8. No
9. 1.7, 3.2
10. $\frac{3}{4}$, $1\frac{1}{2}$
11. double or multiply by 2
12. 750, 900, 1050

Focus test 7

1. right-angled
2. equilateral
3. isosceles
4. true
5.

6. 6
7. *Check that the quadrilateral is symmetrical.*
8.

Name of shape	Number of faces	Number of vertices	Number of edges
Cube	6	8	12
Tetrahedron	4	4	6

9. (triangular) prism, cylinder
10. 6
11.

Type of angle	Acute	Obtuse	Right
Number of angles	1	1	2

12. Angle *a* =135°, Angle *b* =45°

Focus test 8

1.

2. 18 squares
3. 8 cm
4. 36 cm²

5

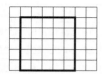

6 24 cm
7 24 cm
8 B
9 120 m²
10 44 m
11 3 cm
12 *Check there is a line between A and C. Check A and B are ticked.*

Focus test 9

1

Metres	Centimetres	Millimetres
6.5 m	**650 cm**	**6500 mm**
7.2 m	720 cm	**7200 mm**
3 m	**300 cm**	3000 mm

2 4800 ml
3 600 g
4 3400 g
5 85 mm, 0.8 m, 85 cm, 8.5 m
6 800 ml or 0.8 litres
7 2500 ml or 2.5 litres
8 37 mm, 25 mm, 4.5 cm
9

10 300 ml
11

12 8:40pm

Focus test 10

1 (−2, 2)
2 (−2, 7)
3 (3, 7)
4

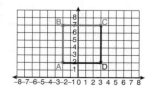

5 (3, 2)
6 *Check the triangle is isosceles with two sides the same length.*
7 *Check the coordinates match the vertices of the triangle drawn.*
8 reflected
9 rotated
10 translated
11 rotated
12 *Check pattern for translation, rotation or reflection.*

Focus test 11

1

	Odd number	Not an odd number
Multiple of 3	21	24
Not a multiple of 3	23 25	22

2 4
3 8
4 17
5

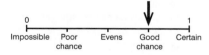

6 12
7 1
8 25
9 7 pints
10 2 litres
11 600 ml
12 5 litres

Focus test 12

1 7 m
2 9 m
3 8 m
4 9 m
5 8 m
6 good chance
7

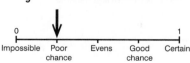

8 poor chance
9

10 1 in 8
11 1 in 2
12 1 in 4

Mixed paper 1

1 3400
2 3910
3 × 10
4 × 100
5 7661
6 3704
7 11.2 kg
8 7.5 km
9 60
10–14

IN	5	3	**4**	9	**7**	8
OUT	30	**18**	24	**54**	42	**48**

15 47
16 49
17 45
18 48
19 $\frac{1}{4}$
20 $\frac{7}{10}$
21 $\frac{1}{2}$
22 $\frac{1}{5}$
23 25
24 191
25–26 160, 200
27–29

Name of shape	Number of faces	Number of vertices	Number of edges
Cuboid	6	8	12

30

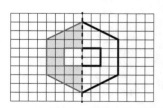

31 63 square centimetres
32 32 cm
33 64 square centimetres
34 32 cm
35 45 mm
36 150 g
37 10:40
38 11:10
39

40 (3, 5)

41

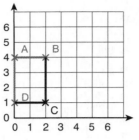

41 (graph showing points A at (3,5) and D at (3,2))

42	South
43	16
44	trees
45	7
46	51
47	6
48	5
49	To have a hot day in July
50	To hear a bird sing

Mixed paper 2

1	0.9
2	0.07
3	8800 m
4	7300 m
5	£15.60
6	£4.40
7	1334
8	3753
9	6878
10	148
11	24 r 2
12	300
13	230
14	34

15–18 (56) 7 18 26 14 (8)

19	75%

20–22 $\frac{1}{20} < \frac{1}{4} < \frac{9}{10}$

23	35
24	293
25	536
26	1

27

28	4
29	prism
30	pyramid
31	100 square centimetres
32	40 cm

33

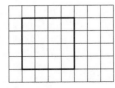

34	16 cm

35–38 65 ml, 600 ml, 6000 ml, 6½ litres
39 (0, 4)
40

(graph showing points A at (0,4), B at (2,4), D at (0,1), C at (2,1))

41 (3, 1)
42

(graph showing a shape with points A at (0,4), B at (2,4), D at (0,1), C at (2,1) and a square from (4,1) to (6,4))

43	35
44	Men's
45	50
46	6
47	8
48	10
49	certain
50	good chance

Mixed paper 3

1	>
2	>
3	3450
4	6012

5–7

+	93	76
48	141	**124**
57	150	**133**

8	67
9	10.4
10	25 g
11	30 km
12	18
13	1.5
14	2.5

15–18

	Multiple of 6	Not a multiple of 6
Factor of 36	18	9
Not a factor of 36	24	13

19–20 $\frac{4}{6}$, $\frac{6}{9}$

21–22

	Greater than ½	Less than ½
0.61	✓	
0.16		✓

23–24	25, 800
25–26	4, 128

27

28–30

	Prism	Not a prism
Has triangular faces	C	B
Has no triangular faces	A	

31	15 m
32	12.4 m
33	A
34	12 cm
35	2 m and 200 cm
36	3500 ml
37	750 g
38	1 kg 500 g
39	rotation
40	translation
41	reflection
42	(3, 0)
43	30 cm
44	6 inches
45	10 inches
46	2.5 cm or 2½ cm
47	40
48	40
49	even chance
50	poor chance

Mixed paper 4

1–4	3.18 < 3.81 < 8.31 < 13.8
5–8	56 and 71, 53 and 38, 37 and 52, 49 and 64
9	28 kg
10	260
11	26
12–13	36 and 45
14	36
15	>
16	<
17–18	15, 5

19–20 (0.05), 0.8

21	75%
22	5%
23–24	16, 49

25 1.5
26 $2\frac{1}{4}$
27–29

Type of angle	Acute	Obtuse	Right
Number of angles	1	2	1

30 6 faces
31 30 cm
32 30 cm
33 A
34

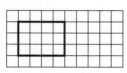

35 2 m
36 2400 g
37 300 ml
38 700 ml
39–40 (−1, 2), (1, 2)
41–42

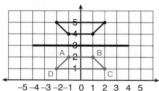

43–46

	Has right angles	Has no right angles
Quadrilateral	A G	C H
Not a quadrilateral	B E	D F

47 30 kg
48 40 kg
49 good chance
50 impossible

Mixed paper 5

1 26.4 m
2 1.5 kg
3 3.7
4 50.2
5 7.5
6 45.1
7 52
8 0.4
9 5114
10 245
11 210
12 23
13 6
14 2

15 11
16 81
17 21
18 51
19 $\frac{2}{3}$
20 $\frac{4}{5}$
21 $\frac{3}{5}$
22 $\frac{3}{10}$
23 1400
24 −5
25 1300
26 14.5
27 acute
28 Angle $z = 130°$
29 cube
30 8 vertices
31 Check there is a line between A and C.
32 Check A and D are ticked.
33 8 cm
34 290 m²
35 18 cm
36 24 cm
37 8000 g
38 4500 ml
39 rotation
40 translation
41 (−3, 4)
42

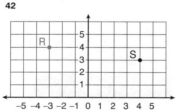

43 Thursday
44 Monday
45 27
46 2
47 5p
48 10p
49 1 in 6
50 1 in 2

Mixed paper 6

1–2 8.08, 10.8
3 63 551
4 72 109
5 2214
6 1259
7–9

```
   3 5 7
 + 2 9 4
   6 5 1
```

10 =
11 <
12 >
13 £88
14 12
15 35
16 6
17 52
18 23 or 29
19 B
20 A
21 C
22 6
23–24 86, 80
25–26 100, 36
27 isosceles
28 Angle $b = 70°$
29

30 4 faces
31 34 cm
32 A and B have the same length perimeter.
33 2 m²
34 48 m²
35 100 ml
36 900 ml
37 3500 g
38 10:55am
39 (5, 0)
40 (0, 2)
41

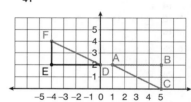

42 rotation
43 2 kg
44 3 months
45 1 kg
46 2–3 months
47 11 cm
48 12 cm
49 1 in 2
50 1 in 4

7 Draw an arrow on this probability scale to show your answer to question 6.

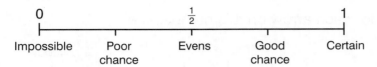

8 What is the chance that the chair you are sitting on will break today? Underline the answer.

impossible   poor chance   even chance   good chance   certain

9 Draw an arrow on this probability scale to show your answer to question 8.

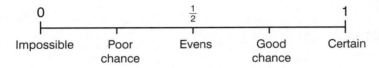

All these 2-D shapes are placed in a bag and one is picked out at random each time, then replaced in the bag.

Write **1 in 2**, **1 in 3**, **1 in 4** or **1 in 8** for each question.

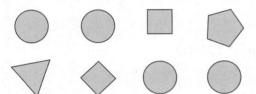

There is a 1 in 4 chance of picking a square: 2 out of 8 shapes.

10 What is the probability of picking a triangle out of the bag? _____

11 What is the probability of picking a circle out of the bag? _____

12 What is the probability of picking either a triangle or a pentagon?

_____

Mixed paper 1

1–2 Write the number for each arrow on this number line.

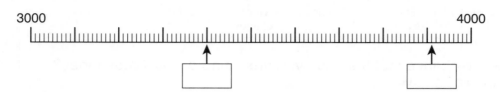

3000   4000

2

Write × **10** or × **100** to make each statement true.

3 14.3 _____ = 143

4 0.5 _____ = 50

2

Complete these calculations.

5   2 9 0 3
   + 4 7 5 8
_____

6   6 5 8 3
   − 2 8 7 9
_____

2

7 What is the total weight of two boxes weighing 3.6 kg and 7.6 kg?
_____ kg

1

8 What is the difference between 4.5 km and 12 km? _____ km

1

9 I am thinking of a number.

If I take away 36 and add 50 the answer is 74.

What is the number I am thinking of? _____

1

10–14 This is a 'multiply by 6' machine. Write the missing numbers in the chart.

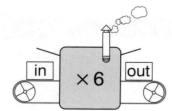

IN	5	3	__	9	__	8
OUT	30	__	24	__	42	__

5

Choose from these numbers to answer each question.

| 45 | 46 | 47 | 48 | 49 | 50 | 51 |

15 Which number is a prime number? _____

16 Which number is a square number? _____

17 Which number is a multiple of 3 and 5? _____

18 Which number has 10 factors, including 1 and itself? _____ ⟨4⟩

19 What fraction of this shape is shaded? Circle the answer.

$\dfrac{1}{2}$ $\dfrac{3}{10}$ $\dfrac{1}{3}$ $\dfrac{1}{4}$ $\dfrac{3}{4}$

⟨1⟩

Write these percentages as fractions in their lowest terms.

20 70% = _____   21 50% = _____   22 20% = _____ ⟨3⟩

23 What is the next square number after 16? _____

24 What is the next odd number after 189? _____ ⟨2⟩

25–26 Write the missing numbers in this sequence.

80   120   _____   _____   240   280 ⟨2⟩

27–29 Complete this chart.

Name of shape	Number of faces	Number of vertices	Number of edges
Cuboid	_____	_____	_____

⟨3⟩

30 Cross out the shape that is **not** a pentagon.

⟨1⟩

29

Calculate the area and perimeter for each of these shapes.

31 Area = _____ square centimetres

32 Perimeter = _____ cm

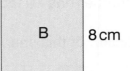

A   7cm

9cm

33 Area = _____ square centimetres

34 Perimeter = _____ cm

B   8cm

4

35 What is the length of this line in millimetres? _____ mm

1

36 What is the most likely weight of an apple? Circle the answer.

5 kg   150 g   1500 g   1 kg   5 g

1

37 What time is shown on this clock? _____

38 What will the time be half an hour later? _____

2

39 Draw the reflection of this shape. The dotted line is the mirror line.

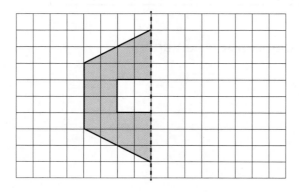

1

40 What are the coordinates of point A? (_____, _____)

41 Point D is at (3, 2). Plot this point and label it.

42 If you stood at point A and faced point D, which direction would you face? Circle your answer.

North   South   West   East

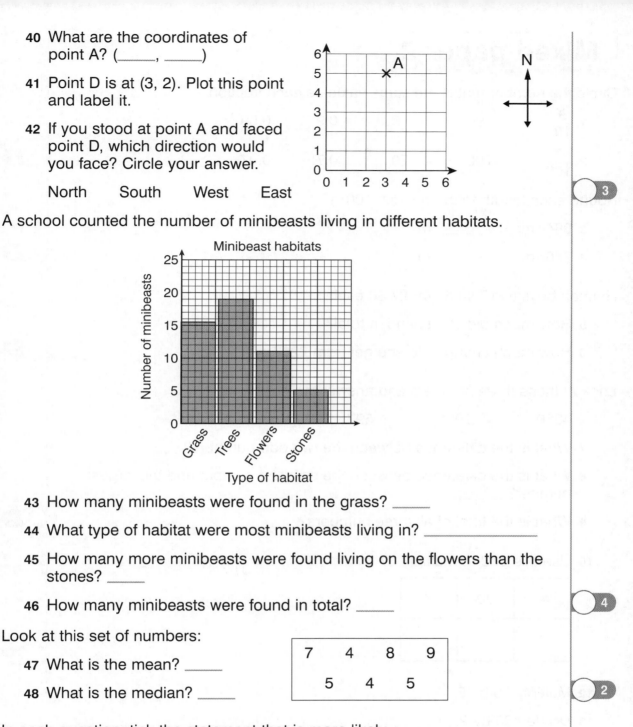

3

A school counted the number of minibeasts living in different habitats.

43 How many minibeasts were found in the grass? _____

44 What type of habitat were most minibeasts living in? _____

45 How many more minibeasts were found living on the flowers than the stones? _____

46 How many minibeasts were found in total? _____

4

Look at this set of numbers:

47 What is the mean? _____

48 What is the median? _____

| 7 | 4 | 8 | 9 |
| 5 | 4 | 5 |

2

In each question, tick the statement that is more likely.

49 To have a hot day in July   OR   To have a hot day in December

50 To hear a bird sing   OR   To hear a roll of thunder

2

Now go to the Progress Chart to record your score!   Total   50

31

Mixed paper 2

Circle the number that is the same value as each fraction.

1 $\frac{9}{10}$ 90   9   0.9   0.09

2 $\frac{7}{100}$ 700   70   0.7   0.07   **2**

Round each length to the nearest 100 m.

3 8844 m   _____ m

4 7266 m   _____ m   **2**

Hannah buys two T-shirts for £7.80 each.

5 How much did she spend in total?   £_____

6 How much change did she get from £20?   £_____   **2**

Look at these three numbers and answer the questions.

     4350   1931   597

7 What is the difference between the two odd numbers? _____

8 What is the difference between the smallest number and the largest number? _____

9 What is the total of all three numbers? _____   **3**

10 Use this grid to multiply 37 by 4.   **11** $3\overline{)74}$ r _____

×	30	7
4		

_____   **2**

12 Multiply 60 by 5. _____

13 Divide 460 by 2. _____

14 Which number between 30 and 35 has a remainder of 2 when divided by 4? _____   **3**

15–18 Circle all the multiples of 4 and underline all the factors of 28.

56   7   18   26   14   8

19 What percentage of this shape is shaded? _____%

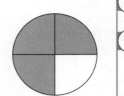

20–22 Write these fractions in order, starting with the smallest.

$\dfrac{9}{10}$ $\dfrac{1}{20}$ $\dfrac{1}{4}$ _____ < _____ < _____

Write the next number in each sequence.

23 47	44	41	38	_____
24 285	287	289	291	_____
25 136	236	336	436	_____
26 0.2	0.4	0.6	0.8	_____

27 Circle the shape that is a hexagon.

28 How many lines of symmetry does a square have? _____

Write the name for each of these shapes: **pyramid** or **prism**.

29

30

_____   _____

What is the area and perimeter of this square?

31 Area = _____ square centimetres

32 Perimeter = _____ cm

10 cm

4

1

3

4

1

1

2

2

33 Draw a square with an area of 16 square centimetres. Use a ruler.

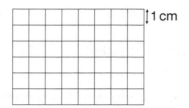

↕1 cm

34 What is the perimeter of the square you have drawn? _____ cm

2

35–38 Write these amounts in order, starting with the smallest.

600 ml   **6½ litres**   **6000 ml**   **65 ml**

_____ , _____   _____   _____

Smallest →

4

39 Write the coordinates of point A. (_____ , _____)

40 Point C is the missing corner of this rectangle at (2, 1). Plot point C and draw two lines to complete the rectangle.

41 Circle the coordinates that are **not** inside the rectangle.

(1, 2)   (3, 1)   (1, 3)

42 Translate the rectangle 4 units east and draw its new position.

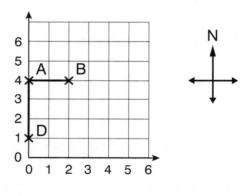

4

This graph shows how many clothes of each type were sold in a shop over one week.

Clothes sales in a week

Types of clothes

Sports
Children's
Women's
Men's

0   10   20   30   40

Number of items sold

43 How many children's clothes were sold in this week? _____

44 Of which type of clothes were 17 items sold? _____

45 How many sports clothes and children's clothes were sold in total?
_____

46 How many more women's clothes than men's clothes were sold?
_____

4

These are David's maths test results.

Monday	Tuesday	Wednesday	Thursday	Friday
7	8	5	10	10

47 What is his mean test result? _____

48 What is his mode test result? _____

2

Underline the chance of each of these things happening.

49 What is the chance that you will blink today?

> impossible   poor chance   even chance
> good chance   certain

50 What is the chance you will go to bed before midnight?

> impossible   poor chance   even chance
> good chance   certain

2

Mixed paper 3

Write < or > to make each number sentence true.

1 9.14 _____ 4.9   **2** 6.08 _____ 0.86   **2**

Read these and write each as a number.

3 three thousand four hundred and fifty _____

4 six thousand and twelve _____   **2**

5–7 Write the missing numbers in this addition grid.

+	93	76
48	141	___
___	150	___

3

8 I am thinking of a number. If I subtract 15 and add 40 my answer is 92.

What number am I thinking of? _____   **1**

9 Work out 36.1 − 25.7 = _____   **1**

10 Three small cakes weigh 75 g. What is the weight of one cake?_____ g   **1**

11 Sam lives 3 kilometres from school. How many kilometres does he travel to and from school in a week, from Monday to Friday?
_____ km   **1**

12 Circle the number that can be divided exactly by 6.

26   20   44   18   52   34   **1**

Circle the correct answer for each of these.

13 $4.5 \div 3 =$ 0.5   0.8   1.5   1.4   2.5

14 $0.5 \times 5 =$ 2   2.5   5   5.2   5.5   **2**

15–18 Write each number in the correct place on this Carroll diagram.

13	24	9	18

	Multiple of 6	Not a multiple of 6
Factor of 36	_____	_____
Not a factor of 36	_____	_____

4

19–20 Complete this equivalent fraction chain.

$$\frac{2}{3} = \frac{4}{\square} = \frac{\square}{9}$$

2

21–22 Use ticks to complete this chart.

	Greater than $\frac{1}{2}$	Less than $\frac{1}{2}$
0.61		
0.16		

2

Write the missing numbers in these sequences.

23–24 _____ 50 100 200 400 _____

25–26 _____ 8 16 32 64 _____

4

27 Circle the shape that is a parallelogram.

1

28–30 Write the letter of each shape in the correct place on this Carroll diagram.

A   B   C

	Prism	Not a prism
Has triangular faces	_____	_____
Has no triangular faces	_____	_____

3

37

A 3.5 m

B 1.2 m

4 m

5 m

31 What is the perimeter of rectangle A? _____ m

32 What is the perimeter of rectangle B? _____ m

33 Which rectangle has the greater area, A or B? _____

34 What is the perimeter of a square with an area of 9 cm²? _____ cm

35 Circle the two measurements that are the same length.

20 mm   2 m   2 km   200 m   200 cm

36 How many millilitres are there in $3\frac{1}{2}$ litres? _____ ml

Write the weight shown on each scale.

37

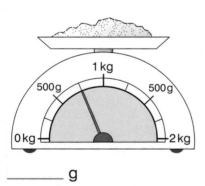

_____ g

38

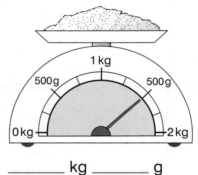

_____ kg _____ g

Write **translation**, **rotation** or **reflection** to describe the movement of the letter A in each of these diagrams.

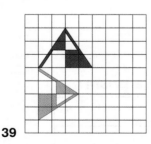

39

_____

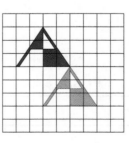

40

_____

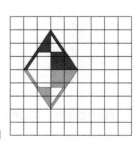

41

_____

42 Circle the coordinates that show the correct position of point Z.

    (3, 1)   (0, 3)   (3, 0)   (1, 3)

This conversion chart shows equivalent lengths in centimetres and inches.

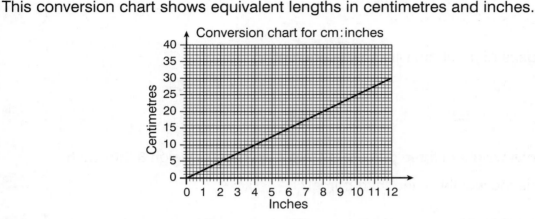

43 When inches were used in schools a ruler was 12 inches long. Approximately how long would the ruler be in centimetres? _____ cm

44 Today some rulers are 15 cm long. Approximately how long would a 15 cm ruler be in inches? _____ inches

45 Which is longer, 10 inches or 10 centimetres? _____

46 Approximately how long is 1 inch? _____ cm

Calculate the mean and median of this set of numbers.

47 Mean = _____

48 Median = _____

40	30	
60	40	30

49 What is the chance of rolling an odd number? Underline the answer.

> impossible   poor chance   even chance
> good chance   certain

50 What is the chance of rolling a 6? Underline the answer.

> impossible   poor chance   even chance
> good chance   certain

Mixed paper 4

1–4 Write this set of decimals in order, starting with the smallest.

    8.31   **13.8**   **3.18**   **3.81**

   _____ < _____ < _____ < _____   **4**

5–8 Join pairs of numbers with a difference of 15.

     56   53   38   37   64

         52   71   49   **4**

9 The total weight of three parcels is 45 kg. Two parcels weigh 8.5 kg each.

What is the weight of the third parcel? _____ kg   **1**

10 Multiply 52 by 5. _____   **11** Divide 78 by 3. _____   **2**

Look at these numbers and answer the questions.

    15   **28**   **36**   **45**

12–13 Which two numbers can be divided exactly by 9? _____ and _____

14 Which number can be divided exactly by both 3 and 4? _____   **3**

Write <, > or = to make each statement true.

15 5^2 _____ 3×8 **16** 9×3 _____ 8^2 **2**

17–18 Write the missing factors for 30.

    $30 \rightarrow$ (1, 30) (2, ____) (3, 10) (____, 6)   **2**

19–20 Circle the smallest decimal and underline the largest decimal.

   0.75   0.5   0.25   0.05   0.8   0.28   **2**

Change these fractions to percentages.

21 $\frac{3}{4} =$ _____%   **22** $\frac{1}{20} =$ _____%   **2**

Write the missing square numbers in this sequence.

23–24 4   9   _____   25   36   _____   64   81   **2**

Write the next number in each sequence.

25 0.3   0.6   0.9   1.2   _____

26 $1\frac{1}{4}$ $1\frac{1}{2}$ $1\frac{3}{4}$ 2   _____

27–29 Look at this kite and complete the chart.

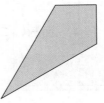

Type of angle	Acute	Obtuse	Right
Number of angles	___	___	___

30 How many faces are there on a cube? _____ faces.

Calculate the perimeter of each rectangle.

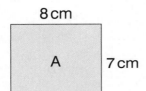

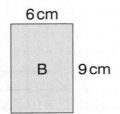

31 Perimeter of A = _____ cm   **32** Perimeter of B = _____ cm

33 Which shape has the larger area, A or B? _____

34 Draw a rectangle on the grid below with a perimeter of 14 cm and an area of 12 square centimetres. Use a ruler.

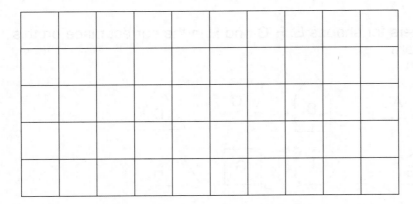

35 What is the most likely height of a door? Circle the answer.

20 cm   2 m   2 km   200 mm

36 Which is heavier, $2\frac{1}{4}$ kg or 2400 g? _____

How much water is there in each jug?

37

1000 ml

500 ml

0

_____ ml

38

1000 ml

500 ml

0

_____ ml

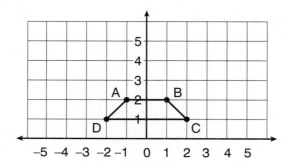

39–40 Circle the coordinates of A and underline the coordinates of B.

(2, −1)   (2, 1)   (−2, 1)   (1, 2)   (−1, 2)   (1, −2)

41–42 Draw a line from (−4, 3) to (4, 3). Use this line as a mirror line and reflect the quadrilateral ABCD.

43–46 Write the letters for shapes E, F, G and H in the correct place on this Carroll diagram.

A

B

C

D

E

F

G

H

	Has right angles	Has no right angles
Quadrilateral	A	C
Not a quadrilateral	B	D

These are the weights of six sacks.

    30 kg   20 kg   90 kg   60 kg   30 kg   10 kg

47 What is the mode weight? _____ kg

48 What is the mean weight? _____ kg

Circle the chance of spinning each number.

49 What is the chance of spinning an odd number?

> impossible   poor chance   even chance
> good chance   certain

50 What is the chance of spinning a 6?

> impossible   poor chance   even chance
> good chance   certain

2

2

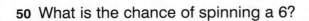
Now go to the Progress Chart to record your score!   Total   50

Mixed paper 5

Round each amount to the nearest tenth.

1 26.38 m   _____ m   **2** 1.54 kg   _____ kg

2

Complete these calculations.

3 37 ÷ 10 =   _____   **4** 5.02 × 10 =   _____

2

Look at these decimal numbers.

    19.2   26.3   18.8   25.7

5 What is the difference between the largest and smallest number?
_____

6 What is the total of the largest and smallest number? _____

7 What is the largest total that can be made from adding any two of these numbers? _____

8 What is the smallest difference that can be made between any two numbers? _____

4

43

Complete these calculations.

9 4935 + 179 = _____

10 49 × 5 = _____

11 7 × 30 = _____

12 92 ÷ 4 = _____

13 36 ÷ 6 = _____

14 What is the remainder when 50 is divided by 3? _____

⬤ 6

Choose from these numbers to answer each question.

11   **21**   **81**   **51**

15 Which number is a prime number? _____

16 Which number is a square number? _____

17 Which number is a multiple of 7? _____

18 Which number has these factors: 1, 3, 17 and itself? _____

⬤ 4

Look at these fractions.

$$\frac{3}{4} \qquad \frac{3}{5} \qquad \frac{2}{3} \qquad \frac{4}{5} \qquad \frac{3}{10}$$

19 Which fraction is equivalent to $\frac{10}{15}$? _____

20 Which fraction has the same value as 80%? _____

21 Which fraction has the same value as 0.6? _____

22 Which fraction is less than $\frac{1}{2}$? _____

⬤ 4

Write the missing number in each sequence.

23 1300   1350   _____   1450   1500

24 5   0   _____   −10   −15

25 1280   1290   _____   1310   1320

26 11.5   13   _____   16   17.5

⬤ 4

44

Look at this quadrilateral.

27 What type of angle is angle *y*?
Circle the answer.

acute   reflex   right   obtuse

28 Use a protractor to measure angle *z* accurately. Angle *z* =_____°

29 What shape will be made when this net
is folded? _____

30 When the net is folded, how many vertices
will the shape have?

_____ vertices

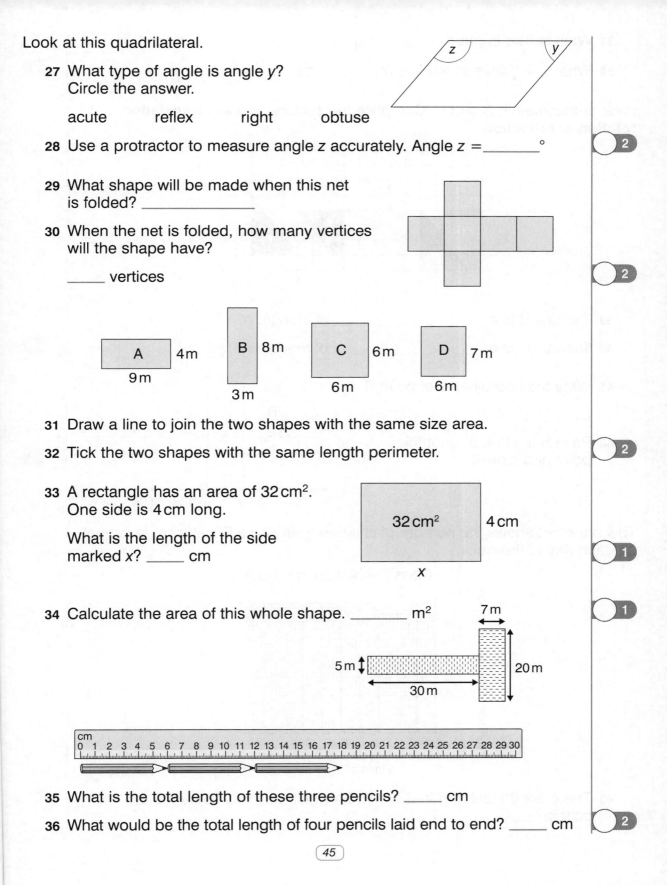

A — 9m × 4m
B — 3m × 8m
C — 6m × 6m
D — 6m × 7m

31 Draw a line to join the two shapes with the same size area.

32 Tick the two shapes with the same length perimeter.

33 A rectangle has an area of 32 cm².
One side is 4 cm long.

What is the length of the side
marked *x*? _____ cm

32 cm²   4 cm
x

34 Calculate the area of this whole shape. _____ m²

7 m
5 m
20 m
30 m

cm
0 1 2 3 4 5 6 7 8 9 10 11 12 13 14 15 16 17 18 19 20 21 22 23 24 25 26 27 28 29 30

35 What is the total length of these three pencils? _____ cm

36 What would be the total length of four pencils laid end to end? _____ cm

45

37 What is 8 kg in grams? _____ g

38 What is $4\frac{1}{2}$ litres in millilitres? _____ ml

2

Look at triangles A, B and C. Complete the sentences using **translation**, **rotation** or **reflection**.

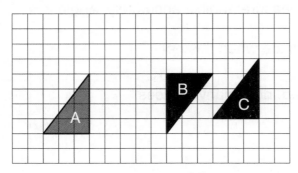

39 Triangle B is a _____ of triangle A.

40 Triangle C is a _____ of triangle A.

2

41 Write the coordinates of point R.

(_____, _____)

42 Point S is at (4, 3). Plot this point and label it.

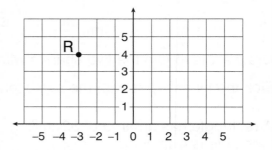

2

This bar chart shows the number of children from Class F that were in school on each day of the week.

Class F: children in school

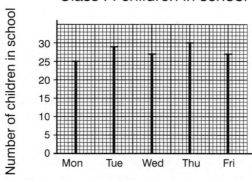

Days of the week

43 There are 30 children in Class F. On which day was everyone at school? _____

46

44 Which day were there five children away from school? _____

45 How many children were in school on Friday? _____

46 How many more children were at school on Tuesday than Wednesday? _____

4

What is the mode and mean of these coins?

47 Mode = _____ p   **48** Mean = _____ p

2

In a bag there are 3 black beads, 2 grey beads and 1 white bead.

49 What is the probability of picking a white bead? Circle the answer.

  1 in 2   1 in 3   1 in 5   1 in 6

50 What is the probability of picking a black bead? Circle the answer.

  1 in 2   1 in 3   1 in 5   1 in 6

2

Mixed paper 6

1–2 Circle the largest number and underline the smallest number in this set.

10.08   8.1   8.08   8.11   10.8   2

Write the number that is 100 more than each of these.

3 63 451   _____

4 72 009   _____   2

5 What is 850 more than 1364?   _____

6 What is 770 less than 2029?   _____   2

7–9 The digits 3, 4 and 5 are missing. Complete this addition by writing the digits in the correct place.

$$\begin{array}{r} \boxed{}\ 5\ 7 \\ +\ \ 2\ \ 9\ \boxed{} \\ \hline 6\ \boxed{}\ 1 \end{array}$$

3

Write =, < or > to make each statement true.

10 $52 \div 4$ _____ 13

11 9×5 _____ 49

12 $81 \div 3$ _____ 26   3

13 Three chairs cost £66. How much will four chairs cost? £_____   1

14 There are 9 balloons in a pack and 4 packs are bought for a party. There is the same number of balloons in 3 different colours.

How many balloons are there of each colour? _____   1

15 Write a multiple of 7 between 30 and 40. _____

16 What is the smallest number that is a multiple of 2 and 3? _____   2

17 $4^2 + 6^2 =$ _____   1

18 Write a **prime number** to make this number sentence true.

20 < _____ < 30

Look at the shaded area on these circles and write the correct letter for each question.

A   B   C   D

19 Which circle has 0.5 shaded? _____

20 Which circle has 70% shaded? _____

21 Which circle has $\frac{3}{5}$ shaded? _____

22 What is $\frac{1}{4}$ of 24? _____

Write the missing numbers in this sequence.

23–24 89 _____ 83 _____ 77 74

25–26 Write the missing square numbers.

_____ 81 64 49 _____

Look at this triangle.

27 What is the name of this triangle?
Underline the answer.

isosceles   equilateral
scalene   right-angled

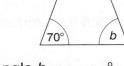

28 Calculate the size of angle *b*. Angle *b* = _____°

29 Circle the net that will make a pyramid when it is folded.

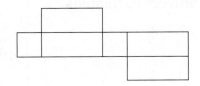 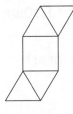 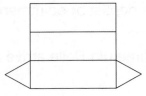

49

30 How many triangular faces are there on a tetrahedron? _____ faces

1

31 A photo is 12 cm by 5 cm wide. A length of wood is used to make a frame for the perimeter of the photo.

What is the length of the wood for this frame? _____ cm

1

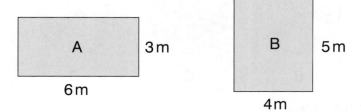

32 Underline the statement that is true.

A has a longer perimeter than B.   B has a longer perimeter than A.

A and B have the same length perimeter.

33 What is the difference in area between rectangles A and B? _____ m²

2

34 What is the area of a room that is 8 m by 6 m? _____ m²

1

35 What is the difference between the amount of liquid in these two jugs? _____ ml

36 What is the total amount of liquid in these two jugs? _____ ml

2

37 2 kg + 1500 g = _____ g

1

38 Belle's dentist appointment was at 11:10am. She arrived 15 minutes early.

What time did Belle arrive at the dentist? _____

1

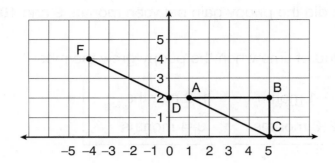

39 Write the coordinates of point C.   (_____ , _____)

40 Write the coordinates of point D.   (_____ , _____)

41 Point E is at (−4, 2). Plot this point and label it.

42 Draw two lines to join D to E and E to F to make a triangle. Underline the word that describes the movement of triangle ABC to the position of triangle DEF.

reflection   rotation   translation

4

This graph shows the weight of a puppy each month in its first year of life.

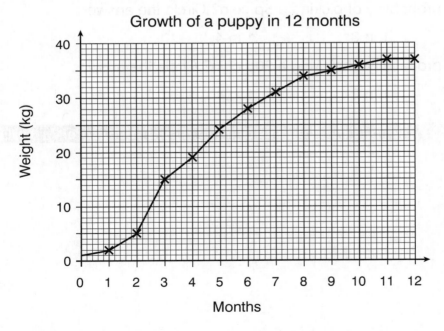

43 How much did the puppy weigh at 1 month old? _____ kg

44 How old was the puppy when it weighed 15 kg? _____ months

45 How much weight did the puppy gain between months 9 and 10?
_____ kg

46 Underline the period of time when the puppy grew the most.

0–1 month	1–2 months
2–3 months	3–4 months

4

Calculate the median and mean of these lengths.

12 cm   9 cm   11 cm   8 cm   20 cm

47 Median length =   _____ cm

48 Mean length =   _____ cm

2

There are four coins in a purse.

49 What is the probability of picking a 5p coin? Circle the answer.

1 in 2   1 in 3   1 in 4

50 What is the probability of picking a 20p coin? Circle the answer.

1 in 2   1 in 3   1 in 4

2

Now go to the Progress Chart to record your score!   Total   **50**